Original title:
Foliage Fragments

Copyright © 2025 Creative Arts Management OÜ
All rights reserved.

Author: Natalia Harrington
ISBN HARDBACK: 978-1-80567-064-3
ISBN PAPERBACK: 978-1-80567-144-2

Reverie in the Leaves

In the park where squirrels dine,
Leaves wave like they're feeling fine.
A gusty breeze does them a favor,
Off they dance, the little paver!

A pumpkin patch in wild disarray,
Hats on heads of greens that sway.
A cabbage rolled, it dreams of fame,
Calling all to join the game!

Rakes are wrestled, lost in jest,
Leaves confetti, all the best!
They tickle noses, whispering tales,
Of cheeky pranks and autumn gales.

But then the wind, it starts to tease,
And whirls the leaves like fussy bees.
A playful whirl, a leafy fight,
In this circus of delight!

The Last Sigh of Summer's Veil

Leaves twirl down with a giggle,
A squirrel's dance turns into a wriggle.
The sun dips low, casting shadows wide,
As pumpkins plot their autumn pride.

The breeze whispers jokes to the trees,
Who chuckle back, swaying with ease.
A final party before the freeze,
Nature's jest in the evening breeze.

Shattered Canopies of Color

Red and gold in a vibrant mess,
A robin tripped; what a funny stress!
As leaves dive-bomb, the world spins bright,
Nature's clowns steal the spotlight.

Branches creak with laughter rare,
Little acorns tumble through the air.
The earth below wears a colorful hat,
As raccoons high-five in a chat.

Echoes of Nature's Tapestry

Whispers of wind play peek-a-boo,
Colored threads stitched on a canvas blue.
Each rustle tells a wacky tale,
Of critters sneaking, setting sail.

Mossy seats where the mushrooms wink,
A frog in a hat begins to drink.
Laughter echoes in the woods each day,
As flora joins in the frolicsome play.

Veils of Green Beneath the Sky

Grassy carpets rolled out wide,
For tiny feet that skip and glide.
Clouds float by, sporting silly hats,
While nature giggles at the spats.

A chameleon hiccups, colors collide,
While daffodils sway, bright and spry.
Underneath the jolly skies they lie,
In this wild dance, oh my, oh my!

Interludes of Decay and Renewal

Amidst the crunch of fallen bliss,
Leaves gossip in the breezy kiss.
They plot a game of hide and seek,
With every rustle, secrets peak.

In the garden, worms hold sway,
Fashioning soil for a grand ballet.
Caterpillars strut in fluff and flair,
While daisies swoon in nature's fair.

Sunflowers nod, with laughter bright,
Chasing bees in a dance of light.
Mushrooms chuckle from the ground,
Adventures underfoot abound.

When winter comes, they'll have their rest,
But springtime calls, it's nature's jest.
So raise your glass to life's grand ruse,
Where nothing's lost, but just amuse.

Symphony of the Departing Right

A leaf took flight, then failed to land,
Met with a squirrel, unexpected band.
They shared a joke, lost in their fun,
As acorns giggled, saying, "Run!"

Dancing branches, all misaligned,
Playing tag, so poorly defined.
Each twist and turn, a stumble here,
Oh look, a pinecone rolling near!

While petals twirl, they tease the breeze,
How often stems just bend their knees.
A serenade of nature's loot,
Where even thorns sport funny suits.

In tangled vines, the laughter clings,
Nature's kids delight in flings.
So let us join this crazy spree,
Life's a laugh; from roots to tree!

Whispers of Autumn Leaves

Golden words in the gentle sway,
Leaves still whisper secrets, come what may.
"Why did the twig refuse to bend?"
"Its stick-to-itiveness became its end!"

A chatty oak in a checkered coat,
Told a tale of a quirky goat.
It laughed so hard, down came its crown,
No dignity left, just a leafy frown.

The breezes cheer, the tales unfold,
As amber hues of stories bold.
They flip and flop, it's quite a show,
Autumn's humor steals the glow.

Each gust of wind spins tales anew,
With chuckles that bring out the hue.
So grab a seat, enjoy the tease,
For nature's rot is quite the breeze!

Echoes of the Canopy

Up above, the branches chatter,
Why do squirrels scurry with such a patter?
One cheeky nut thief on the chase,
Leaves roll their eyes at his wild race.

Beneath the boughs, the shadows play,
A dance of light in bright display.
Creek gurgles jokes, the roots all grin,
For life below is where laughs begin.

As sunlight fades, the crickets sing,
With leafy friends in the evening swing.
"Did you hear? The sun still tries!"
While twinkling stars quirk in the skies.

Lush laughter echoes from branch to ground,
In nature's humor, joy is found.
So hold your cup to this merry spree,
For even limbs just want to be free!

Ghosts of Gnarled Roots

In the woods where shadows creep,
Twisted toes curl, in slumber deep.
Old leaves whisper, secrets full,
As squirrels plot their nutty pull.

Mossy chairs for ghosts to lounge,
They giggle behind every branchy crouch.
With acorn hats and wisdom old,
They dance in circles, stories bold.

Beneath the moon, the mischief flies,
Barked complaints from the ancient sighs.
The roots intertwine, yarns unfold,
Their tales have grown a bit too bold.

Now watch the tricksters, one and all,
As roots make mischief, hear them call.
With every twist, they laugh and tease,
Oh, to join their leafy breeze!

Chasing Shadows Beneath

A shady dance on summer's ground,
Where sunlight kisses with a sound.
Step right over that patch of gloom,
Watch out for the shadow's zoom!

Barefoot chases, a wild spree,
Bumping into roots with glee.
Trip and tumble, then a laugh,
Who knew shadows had a path?

Leaves like masks, they play hide and seek,
With every rustle, they're not so meek.
A tickling breeze throws leaves around,
Nature's jesters, never found.

Giggles rise with the breaking dawn,
As trees stretch tall in a leafy yawn.
Running under this green brigade,
Life's a game, no need for shade!

The Heartbeat of the Earth

Pulsing whispers in the dirt,
Dancing worms in their shy shirt.
Insects bumble with a cheer,
Tickle the soil, lend an ear!

The thumping roots keep secrets low,
While daisies giggle in a row.
Every heartbeat forms a joke,
As daisies tease the stubborn oak.

Beneath the surface, laugh and play,
With nature's rhythm, join the fray.
Rumbling roots and sprightly twirls,
Laughing softly, the underworlds.

A raucous roar, a gentle hum,
Comes from life, hear the drum.
In the soil, where the fun is set,
Let's dance, dear friend, with no regret!

Segments of Serenity

Tiny leaves in a sunny patch,
Like little flags on a nature latch.
Softly swaying, they plot and scheme,
Whispering secrets, living the dream.

A splintered twig, a cheeky prick,
Reminds us morning comes with a trick.
Pinecones giggle as they roll,
Treefolk chuckle, aiming for a goal.

Sunbeams beam, a silly sight,
Casting shadows, causing flight.
Come join the fun, it's quite absurd,
In the calm, hear chaos stirred.

Laughter spills from branches high,
Beneath the boughs, we all comply.
Segments of joy in this leafy cheer,
Nature's laughter, always near!

Tapestry of Green

In the garden, a leaf did dance,
Twisting and twirling, taking a chance.
With a wink to the flower, it said, "Look at me!"
While bees buzzed around, sipping their tea.

A squirrel joined in, with a floppy hat,
Gossiping loudly 'bout his favorite spat.
"Did you see the sun? He's shining too bright!"
They all cracked up, it was quite a sight!

Shattered Shades of Nature

The tree limbs chuckled, branches all bent,
Sharing tall tales of where the wind went.
One said, "I swayed, nearly lost my bark!"
The one next to him replied, "That's a lark!"

A fallen acorn said, with great pride,
"I'm a nut, not just any. I'm bona fide!"
While mushrooms giggled, growing on the side,
Whispering secrets that they could not hide.

Leafy Secrets Unraveled

Leaves in the breeze, playing peekaboo,
Waving at passersby, 'Hey, how are you?'
One leaf got bold, suggested a game,
While the others just chuckled, not one felt the same.

"Let's dress up as flowers, it'll be a blast!"
Said a bold little sprout, eager and fast.
But the daisies just sighed, "You won't pull it off,
Your shorts and your style? Oh please, just scoff!"

When Petals Speak

Petals began chattering under a sunbeam,
"Do you think we're fancy? Or just part of a dream?"
One rose replied, "I like my fragrance fine,
But you lot should cool it, you're straddling the line!"

A daffodil laughed, "Let's host a parade!"
While tulips just twirled, in colors arrayed.
"Right now," said a daisy, "let's take a seat,
Listen to the grass, isn't it sweet?"

Silhouettes of Seasons Past

Leaves in shades of orange glow,
Whispers of a warm breeze flow.
Squirrels prepping for a feast,
Cackling like they're hosting least.

Branches bow under their weight,
As nutty chatter seals their fate.
Rustle and tumble, too much fun,
Nature's histrionics have begun.

Each branch a tale, it seems they tell,
Of autumn escapades, oh so swell.
A dance of shadows, a rustling spree,
Silly silhouettes, just wait and see!

Time's footprints fade, in twirls of cheer,
The forest giggles, can you hear?
Seasons past, with laughter entwined,
Echoes of joy, forever combined.

Rustling Remnants of the Forest

In the canopy, a rustling tune,
Leaves gossip beneath the moon.
Critters creep with stealthy glee,
A party's brewing—join with me!

Crickets chirp like childlike clowns,
While owls wear their sleepy frowns.
Branches sway with comic grace,
Nature's jesters put on a face.

A tumble of twigs, a shuffle of cones,
Even the pine has ticklish tones.
The forest floor, a stage of gags,
Where laughter echoes and no one lags.

In every crack, the chuckles bloom,
Mischievous roots in every room!
Every rustle, a joke to unwind,
A comedy show that nature designed.

Petals in a Dance with Time

Petals flutter like silly sprites,
Spinning 'round in dizzy flights.
Bumblebees buzz with giddy zest,
Joining in on this fluff-filled jest.

A daisy laughs, a rose giggles,
While dandelions twist and wiggle.
Nature's ball, with blooms in line,
A pastel waltz, oh how they shine!

Winds of whimsy tease the flowers,
In a conga line that never sours.
Each petal toss, a giggly fling,
Chasing moments, a joyous spring.

Old times tumble in a floral spree,
As fragrance twirls in harmony.
Time's petals flutter, but what a sight,
Dancing blooms in pure delight!

Reflections on Mossy Memories

Mossy pads like green velvet seats,
Nature hosts its comfy feats.
Toadstools gather, a whimsical crew,
With chuckling echoes—who knew?

Underfoot, the squishy ground,
Imprints of giggles, so profound.
A twig snaps with a hint of glee,
As laughter bubbles up from the tree.

Reflections on what's grown over time,
Each ring on a trunk, a nursery rhyme.
With gnarled roots weaving tall tales,
The forest chuckles, echoing trails.

In the shadows, memories blend,
Adventures captured, never to end.
Mossy carpets hold stories bright,
Where nature's humor takes its flight.

Wild Whispers in the Dappled Light

In the woods, a squirrel prances,
Gathering nuts, it takes its chances.
Dancing shadows, cheeky sprites,
Crackling laughter in the green delights.

A rabbit hops, a toadstool hat,
Waving hello, how about that?
Wind tickles leaves, secrets to share,
Rustling giggles fill the air.

The sunbeams drop like lazy flies,
As critters plot their sunny lies.
A fox in shades, so suave and neat,
Calls the dance floor, oh what a feat!

Here in the shade, the fun won't stop,
Nature's circus, a leafy shop.
Jokes from branches, laughter rings,
Ah, the wild has such wild things!

The Art of Leaves Unraveled

Leaves like handkerchiefs swirl and spin,
Playing games where the fun begins.
A flurry of colors, a jester's play,
Whispers of joy in the autumn ballet.

A chipmunk, so silly, in a leaf pile dives,
Careful not to scare the butterflies' lives.
With a splash and a tumble, oh what a sight,
Leaves fly high, oh what pure delight!

Branches gossip about the falling hues,
Chirping about morning news.
The sun winks down, a playful tease,
As shadows dance, like mischievous bees.

Under the canopy where whispers delight,
Nature's humor takes its flight.
Around every bend, a chuckle awaits,
In this leafy world, joy creates!

Beneath the Canopy's Gentle Hold

A bear in the brush has lost his way,
Stumbling and tumbling, oh what a display!
He trips on roots and snags upon vines,
But laughs off the chaos, oh how he shines!

The owl hoots softly, wise and old,
Murmurs sweet secrets, softly told.
While a wisecracking crow caws with flair,
Plucking at leaves, without a care.

A playful breeze stirs up the show,
Tickling the branches, just so you know.
As laughter drips from the trees on high,
Nature's joke book, oh me, oh my!

Under the green, where giggles unfold,
Every whisper is cheeky and bold.
So come take a stroll in this funny land,
Where nature paints joy with a playful hand!

Nature's Manuscript of Changing Hues

Once was a leaf with dreams untold,
It wished to be bright and vivid gold.
A gust came by, it twirled and spun,
Now it's a kite, oh what fun!

Foliage tales in colors vast,
Green meets amber, the die is cast.
Blushing reds and oranges in a row,
Like a comedy act, they steal the show.

A wind-up squirrel in a leafy suit,
Tells jokes about a playful root.
Nutty punchlines and acorn glee,
Making each moment a laugh spree.

So here's to the pages, a frolicsome spread,
Where nature pens laughs on a silken thread.
With chuckles and grins in this vibrant space,
Every leaf shares a smile, a happy face!

Leaves of Time

In the park, a leaf took flight,
It swirled and danced, oh what a sight!
A squirrel yelled, "Hey, that's not fair!"
The leaf just giggled, floating in air.

A breeze came by, it blew so strong,
The leaf chatted back, "You can't be wrong!"
"Without us leaves, trees look quite bare,"
The tree just chuckled, full of flair.

With every rustle, they made their point,
"We're the wise ones, come take a joint!"
But when it rained, they all turned beige,
The trees all shook, and laughed in rage.

So next time you see a leaf's delight,
Remember the fun that's hidden from sight,
For in their whispers, secrets are found,
Nature's jesters, spinning around.

Arboreal Dreams

Up in the branches, a dream took form,
A tree that juggled in a lightning storm.
The berries laughed as they bounced down,
The roots held on, wearing a crown.

"Y'all think you're sharp? Just look at my bark!"
The oak stretched out and set off a spark.
The pine responded, "I smell a joke!"
While the maples just shimmer and cloak.

At midnight, they held a dance on the lawn,
With shadows prancing until the dawn.
But when dawn broke, oh what a scene!
A sleepy dog lied, dreaming of green.

So next time you nap under leafy glades,
Remember the fun that nature parades.
For in the trees, laughter still gleams,
In their secret world of arboreal dreams.

Tints of Time's Passage

Colors shift as seasons tease,
Grass gets lazy, swaying with ease.
Each petal whispers tales of the past,
While daisies giggle, dancing so fast.

A poke from a branch brings such surprise!
With a wink and a nod, it tries to disguise.
Colors parade, marching through air,
"Fetch us some water! We want some flair!"

The sun goes low, a painter at play,
In hues of orange, golds, and gray.
Each leaf has a story, some wild and absurd,
While the breeze hums soft, saying a word.

So here's to the tinting, the laugh, and the morn,
To nature's array, where humor is born.
For in every shade, in each fleeting glance,
Time plays its hand in a comical dance.

Nature's Curious Collage

In the woods, an artist convenes,
Creating a masterpiece of greens.
With twigs as pencils and leaves as paint,
A critter exclaimed, "Now this is quaint!"

A rabbit hopped in, with a brush on its ear,
Scribbling sunshine, oh so sincere.
While ants carried frames, aligning with pride,
Each stroke an adventure, each leaf, a guide.

A wind chime giggled from the old oak tree,
"I'm more artful than you'll ever be!"
But the mushrooms just chuckled, "We add the flair,
With spots and colors that dance in the air."

So take a moment, look close, and see,
Nature's collage, its own jubilee.
For in every creation, a tale will emerge,
A whimsical dance, where all things converge.

Latticework of Leafy Lyricism

In the garden, a tumbleweed,
Whispers jokes to the bumblebee.
A squirrel snickers at my hat,
Where's the punchline? Oh, it sat!

Leaves pretending to hold a conference,
Debating who gets to wear the essence.
The oak laughs, boasting it's grand,
While ivy giggles, stretching its hand.

A caterpillar in a bow tie,
Cracks a joke as it crawls by.
Chirpy crickets join the cheer,
This is nature's stand-up, dear!

With each rustling, they share a tale,
Of mishaps involving a snail's trail.
The twigs chuckle, all in good cheer,
Life's punchline is always near!

The Silence Between Branches

In the trees, a secret giggle,
As branches dance and softly wiggle.
An acorn jokes, 'I'm not a nut!'
But every squirrel gives a big strut!

Leaves play hide and seek with the sun,
Whispering stories, oh what fun!
A bird chirps, 'I've lost my key!'
Maybe it flew off in a spree!

Twigs pretending to be a band,
With raccoons as fans, so unplanned.
While shadows pass, a leaf falls low,
Did that leaf just steal the show?

A standoff of sorts, who's got the best look?
A peacock feather, they all took.
The forest chuckles in quiet delight,
As leaves wear crowns, oh what a sight!

Harvest of the Forgotten Woods

In a patch where mushrooms bloom,
Frogs croak jokes that dispel gloom.
A mouse pulls out a giant cheese,
Squeaking, 'Dinner's up, if you please!'

The harvest moon shines, wise and bright,
Chasing shadows, what a sight!
A raccoon swipes a candy bar,
Yells, 'Next round's on me, not far!'

Wandering through a thicket dense,
Came upon a scarecrow hence.
He grins with a pitchfork held tight,
Said, 'Don't pluck my crops, or get a fright!'

Bouncing squirrels join the spree,
Planning pranks with acorns, you see.
In this woodland fiesta, they reign supreme,
Turning everyday life into a dream!

Fragments of Green Beneath My Feet

Stepping lightly on leafy streams,
Where blades of grass tell funny memes.
A worm wriggles, slipping and sliding,
Says, 'No place for you, I'm hiding!'

The ground chuckles as I walk by,
Poking fun as if to say hi.
'Watch your step!' the daisies cheer,
'We know how to tickle from here!'

Each pebble feels like a comedian's joke,
As dandelions puff out, smoke!
The snippets of green laugh aloud,
'Step here, my friend, make us proud!'

Fragments all gather in a whirl,
Nature's confetti in a twirl.
Creating moments so sweet and neat,
Life is joy beneath my feet!

Stories in the Bark

Once I tried to climb a tree,
Chasing squirrels, just to see.
I slipped and fell, barked my knee,
Now I talk to trees like they're free.

Their gnarled features, sly and wry,
Whisper tales of days gone by.
Lost a shoe, oh me, oh my!
Now raccoons have quite a guy.

The trunk's a library of my clumsiness,
Every scratch a tale of fun and mess.
I read them daily, I confess,
In bark's embrace, I find no stress.

So when you walk among the trees,
Remember stories on the breeze.
And when you trip, just laugh with ease,
Nature's here to spread its tease.

Beneath the Surface of Green

Oh, what a dance beneath the leaves,
Where ants plot schemes and daylight weaves.
I saw a worm, dressed like a king,
While crickets held a summery fling.

A ladybug adorned in red,
Tells gossip of the flower bed.
A dandelion swayed with grace,
While laughing at the snail's slow pace.

In muddy puddles, critters dive,
With belly flops, they come alive.
And mushrooms giggle, puffing smoke,
As tree frogs croak their finest joke.

So peek beneath that verdant dome,
Find hidden glee that likes to roam.
In nature's laughter, we feel at home,
Come join the party; you're not alone.

The Hymn of the Hues

Oh, purple leaves on orange trees,
Dance like they're riding on the breeze.
The yellow blooms are cracking jokes,
While green-tongued frogs have ribbeting folks.

Red berries sing in quirky tune,
While grasses sway and curly groom.
The sun's a painter with a brush,
Creating chaos in the hush.

Blue butterflies take daring leaps,
Over petals where the humor creeps.
Each color laughs in vibrant cheer,
Unfolding nature's funny sphere.

So join the hymn of hues so bright,
Where every shade brings pure delight.
In nature's palette, feel the light,
And find your laughter in plain sight.

Tangled in Nature's Embrace

I got lost in a tangle of vines,
Thought I'd find freedom, instead I twine.
A cheeky spider threw me a wink,
Said, "Join the party, come have a drink!"

The grass tickles my toes with glee,
As I tumble down, oh, can't you see?
With flowers laughing in the sun,
Nature's embrace is full of fun.

A hedgehog waved, "I'm doing fine!"
While bees bumbled in a straight line.
I danced with daisies, spun in place,
Tangled in laughter, a wild embrace.

So if you wander, don't be shy,
Let thorns and twigs be your alibi.
In nature's grip, we love to play,
Join the chaos, come what may!

Stories in the Stratum

Leaves gossip in the breeze,
Telling tales of tree's unease.
Squirrels roll their eyes so wide,
As acorns dance, and branches glide.

A thistle had a daring plan,
To serenade a frightened man.
He tripped on roots, oh what a sight,
A comedy, in morning light.

Old moss claims he's quite the sage,
With secrets hidden page by page.
He chuckles at a tulip's woes,
For it can't keep up with prose.

In soil, the worm has tales to weave,
Of dreams the petals can't believe.
A fairy thinks she's on a quest,
But lands in leaves—oh, what a pest!

The Spirit of Renewal

A sprout burst forth with lots of glee,
"Look at me! I'm fancy-free!"
A daisy scoffed, "You're just a sprig,
One storm away from doing a jig!"

The grass whispered to a sneaky weed,
"Your boldness is quite a brazen creed!"
While daisies swayed with all their charm,
To keep the soil from getting warm.

The branches shivered in the wind,
As snoring roots at dusk rescind.
They joined a dance, a leafy troupe,
Beneath the moon, a silly loop.

In the cracks, the flowers found,
A treasury of beauty, unbound.
With laughter echoing far and wide,
In riotous colors, nature's pride.

Whispers Among the Vines

Vines entwined with gossip grand,
"Did you see the peach take a stand?"
"He flaunts his fuzz, but look, he's small,
A little creature, after all!"

The ivy snickered, wrapped up tight,
"Oh, don't you dare draft in the night!"
As voles peeked out, oh such a show,
Swinging on tendrils, putting on a pro!

A tendril quipped, "Life's quite absurd,
With all these critters, haven't you heard?"
Yet who can blame, when fruits parade,
As bustling bugs dance in the shade?

They teamed up for a leafy feast,
Bright berries grasped, at least!
Nature's banquet, full of cheer,
Turning whispers into roars of jeer!

Hidden Narratives in Green

In emerald hues where secrets sleep,
Where raindrops giggle and shadows peep.
The rustling leaves, oh what a crew,
Narrate adventures, winks from dew!

A dandelion's quest was bold,
To conquer all with threads of gold.
But bees had plans to chase him off,
And in the sun, his dreams scoff!

The ferns had stories, tall to tell,
But only whispered among their shell.
In their green arms, tales would clench,
Of battles fought, and rumbles wrench.

The shadows rolled as twists unfold,
While clovers giggle, brave and bold.
A wishbone moment in the glade,
Leaves laugh, as moments softly fade!

The Hidden Life Beneath

In the dirt, a party's on,
Worms are dancing till the dawn.
Mice are playing hide and seek,
While the roots try not to sneak.

Tiny bugs in tiny hats,
Throwing crumbs for tiny rats.
Mole's got jokes, he makes them laugh,
While ants take turns with a photograph.

A gopher guzzles his carrot cake,
In this world, they all partake.
Squirrels wonder where they went,
Did they steal that pie? They just might have meant!

Underneath, the fun prevails,
Nature's jokes tell wondrous tales.
A secret life, so full of glee,
Where everyone's as happy as can be!

A Cascade of Colors

Leaves are falling like a show,
Spinning 'round in vibrant flow.
Red and gold, a funny sight,
They trip and tumble, what a flight!

Squirrels giggle at the dance,
As acorns roll, they take a chance.
Pumpkins grinning, orange cheer,
Wondering when they'll disappear!

Wind whispers 'catch me if you can,'
As twirling veggies hatch a plan.
Lettuce rolls, and carrots race,
Who knew greens possessed such grace?

In this riot of hues, they play,
Not a single frown today.
Join the chaos, feel the spin,
Where all the laughter does begin!

Green Echoes in Stillness

In the quiet, rustles grow,
Whispers caught in a green flow.
A snail declared it's time to feast,
While beetles clapped, to say the least.

Frogs pitched in a croaky song,
To see who'd sing the loudest wrong.
Grasshoppers hopped in merry glee,
Trying to mimic a bumblebee.

Leaves chuckle at the hush,
As the daisies start to blush.
Every still moment, a joke surmised,
Nature's lullaby, so aptly disguised.

With each echo, laughter reigns,
Life's little quirks flow through the veins.
In the calm, they find delight,
A funny twist in the dimming light!

Undercurrents of Soil

Underneath the surface deep,
Critters plot, and secrets keep.
Grubs are pranking, throwing dirt,
While mushrooms snicker, 'Ain't this hurt?'

Roots are tangled in a tease,
Whispering tales to the buzzing bees.
They share jokes in earthy tones,
While rocks just grin, like old-time bones.

Potatoes roll in grand parade,
In a rooty escapade they've made.
"Oh, is it time for dinner now?"
They wonder, while all take a bow!

Within the womb of earth and muck,
Nature's whimsy brings great luck.
A land of laughter starts to bloom,
With every crevice, joy finds room!

Reflections in the Woods

Squirrels in tuxedos dance with glee,
While owls read poetry from a tree.
A rabbit with glasses, so dapper and neat,
Offers advice on how to treat a beet.

The trees gossip softly when no one's around,
Sharing the secrets of what they have found.
A frog wears a crown, quite regal and proud,
Croaking out laughter, drawing in a crowd.

Beneath the Leafy Veil

Under the leaves, a party unfolds,
With ants serving snacks, as the sunlight scolds.
The beetles play cards, quite into the night,
While fireflies flash, turning dark into light.

A cat with a hat joins the fun by mistake,
Chasing her tail, what a sight to partake!
A raccoon DJ spins some groovy old tunes,
While racquets made of twigs play ball with raccoons.

Visions in Verdant Hues

Green goblins giggle as they plot their pranks,
Sneaking up silently, then giving out janks.
A watermelon floats down a babbling brook,
While turtles play chess with each other's old books.

A snail slides by saying, 'I'm late, can't you see?'
Dressed up in slime, what a sight to decree!
The colorful flowers all roll their big eyes,
As daisies say gossip, and thorns share their lies.

Nature's Forgotten Corners

There's a lost sock tangled in vine and confusion,
And a shoe that's become part of earth's grand fusion.
A gnome with a beard full of moss and of grit,
Complains that the garden is not quite a hit.

The hedgehogs debate if they should go soft,
Or declare they're tough with their prickly loft.
The mushrooms hold meetings about how to play,
As the sun sets high, ending a quirky day.

Whispers of Autumn Leaves

A leaf spoke to a squirrel,
"Is it me, or is it getting colder?"
The squirrel just laughed out loud,
"At least we won't need a boulder!"

Piles of leaves began to dance,
Two ants clumsily pranced.
They slipped and slid on Leafy Lane,
"Next time, let's just stick to rain!"

A crisp breeze took a humble turn,
As noisy seeds began to churn.
They giggled at the ground below,
"Hey, wait up! We want the show!"

Crispy snacks fell from the trees,
An acorn shouted, "What a tease!"
The critters gathered for a feast,
As nature's party grew increased!

Tattered Greens on the Breeze

The dandelions had a showdown,
Shouting, "Can you spin, you crown?"
Wobbling leaves joined in the fun,
"Watch us swirl! We're second to none!"

A butterfly in a wild chase,
Landed right on a silly face.
The grass blades giggled with delight,
"Look at that! It's quite a sight!"

One leaf said, "I feel so old,"
But wisps of wind made it bold.
"Just look at me, I'm kinda free!"
"Embrace the breeze, be wild and carefree!"

Through the garden, laughter rang,
A silly frog began to sang.
"Who knew being green could be this fun?
Now, let's race, it's just begun!"

Mosaic of Nature's Palette

In the park, a canvas wide,
Nature's brush strokes did collide.
A poky rose tossed out a joke,
As daisies chuckled, "What a bloke!"

Colors splashed from green to red,
A sunbeam touched the flowerbed.
"Hey, tulip, wear my shade of gold!"
The flowers cried, "You're being bold!"

Crickets chirped a silly tune,
Dancing 'neath the watchful moon.
"Can we paint the stars a hue?
Let's color every laugh we drew!"

The branches swayed, a gentle tease,
"Hey, gardener, mind the breeze!"
As blossoms burst into a show,
Each scent a laugh, a fragrant glow!

In the Shadow of Withering Vines

A grape whispered, "I'm losing sheen,"
To a pumpkin sporting a smile keen.
"Don't fret, friend, let's start a trend,
Let's roll with weird, let giggles blend!"

In tangled vines, a spider weaved,
A web of jokes, quite deceived.
"Catch my humor, it's quite a trap,
Just watch your step, or take a nap!"

A plucky rose began to pout,
"Why do we never hear a shout?"
"Just wait till fall," said sly old thyme,
"All will laugh—quite a silly rhyme!"

So shadows danced in evening light,
Withered vines embraced the night.
Together they laughed their points of view,
Nature's quirks, a funny hue!

Entwined Narratives

In the park, a squirrel's plan,
To steal a snack from an old man.
He leaps with flair, it's quite a show,
Then lands on flowers, oh no, oh no!

With petals dancing in the breeze,
The man just laughs, and gives a tease.
"Those seeds are mine, you cheeky chap!"
But off he goes, no time for tap!

The trees are witness, old and wise,
To nutty thrills and clever lies.
They whisper tales in rustling tone,
Of treasures hid, and seeds well sown.

So laughter echoes through the leaves,
As nature plays and senses tease.
Each bud and branch tells a jest,
In this green world, we're all a guest.

Trees Speak in Silence

Two birches gossip by the stream,
About a fox who loves to dream.
"Last night he danced on moonlit grass,
And swiped my lunch; the furry rascal!"

The oak, he chuckles, wise and grand,
"Why don't you join his merry band?
A waltz with nature, oh so spry,
Or just swap stories, you'll surely fly!"

The winds, they carry tales of cheer,
From leafy branches, far and near.
Laughter travels, just like a tune,
Under the gaze of the chuckling moon.

Though trunks may be quiet, roots entwine,
In whispered secrets, humor's divine.
For even trees with bark so stout,
Can giggle at life, and dance about!

Flutters of Flora

Petals pirouette in the sky,
While bees buzz by with a blissful sigh.
A dandelion's giggle, a bright yellow jest,
Catching the wind for a pollen-filled quest.

Buds burst open with flowers so bright,
Each one a joke in the morning light.
A daisy winks, a rose gives a grin,
Nature's comedy show, let the fun begin!

The daisies gather for a fun debate,
Who's the prettiest, oh isn't it late?
While violets roll their eyes in glee,
"Why not just bloom and let us be free?"

In this garden of laughter and cheer,
Every blade of grass has a story to share.
With color and chuckles, nature's grand play,
They invite us all to dance and sway!

Merging Past and Present

An old tree's trunk can tell a tale,
Of times gone by, of winds, and gales.
It creaks and groans with each step taken,
A voice so rich, it cannot be shaken.

A curious squirrel scampers up high,
Chasing a leaf that flutters by.
"Catch me, if you can!" the leaf shouts with glee,
While the tree just chuckles, "Oh, let it be!"

Roots weave stories of days long past,
Of storms that came and shadows cast.
Yet here it laughs, in the sunny light,
Creating new tales, all shining bright.

The harmony of old and new blend,
As the laughter of trees will always transcend.
With every season, a new jest is found,
In the quirky dance of the green-filled ground.

Illuminated in Green

A plant on my desk does a jig,
Its leaves wiggling, oh so big.
It sways and chirps in morning's light,
I swear it dances, what a sight!

With potter's clay and dirt-laden shoes,
I found my green friend, a little confused.
It flicks me off with a leafy hiss,
Who knew plants could be such a bliss?

Rivals in the garden, all in the fray,
Competing for sun, oh what a ballet!
A caterpillar slinks past with flair,
Claiming, "The sun's too bright, I swear!"

In this leafy disco, we all rave,
Throwing shade at bugs, the misbehave.
With each snip and each new sprout,
We laugh 'til we fall, there's no doubt!

Sentinels of the Seasons

Oh mighty trees with arms out wide,
You wave at me like a leafy guide.
In spring you push out your greenest wear,
Summer's gown—each branch a flair!

Autumn whispers, 'Let's drop some gold,'
Leaves tumbling down, like stories told.
But winter sighs with a frosty wink,
'Not so fast, let's sip some drink!'

Each season's antics, what a jest,
Nature's humor, and we're the guests.
A squirrel chases as if in a race,
Slips on a leaf, oh what a face!

So stand tall, dear trees, with laughter loud,
You're the punchlines, we feel so proud.
Nature's jesters, forever spry,
We cheer you on 'neath the wide blue sky!

Nature's Storybook Waiting

In the quiet woods, a tale unfolds,
Leaves like pages, some weathered, some bold.
A squirrel writes stories with every hop,
And in the shadows, the mushrooms plop!

The flowers giggle in vibrant hues,
Sharing secrets, exchanging dues.
'You blossom here, I bloom just there,'
'Let's trade places, if you dare!'

A crow caws loudly, a critic indeed,
'Your stories are silly, they lack some speed!'
But the wise old oak just chuckles back,
'Nature's stories are never on track!'

So let the pages flutter in glee,
As the critters share their rhymes with me.
In this book of green, I take my pause,
To join the laughter and cheer for our cause!

Sprouting Whispers of Change

Tiny seeds peeking with curious eyes,
Their whispers echo, beneath open skies.
'What's our fate? Will we bloom or lounge?'
They giggle, dreaming of colors to scrounge!

Each sprout arises with a playful nudge,
'Come on, brave roots, let's really judge!'
Together we'll rise, let's all make a scene,
In this green playground, we'll be evergreen!

A dandelion puffs, 'I'm ready to fly!'
With a whoosh, it bursts, oh my, oh my!
The wind takes charge, laughs in the air,
Leaves twirl around, what a grand affair!

So let's have a party, all greens invited,
Nature's wild dance, utterly delighted.
With each sprout, each giggle, we'll share this day,
For life is a jest, in the best kind of way!

The Dialogue of Decay

In the garden, leaves debate,
"Why'd you fall? Did it feel great?"
One says, "I caught a chilly breeze,
While dodging squirrels and sneezing trees!"

Another chimes, "I wish to prance,
But now I'm stuck without a chance!"
A tumble here, a twisty roll,
And soon enough, they lose control!

"Let's start a band, we'll call it rust!"
One whispered slyly, sensing trust.
The rhythm's fresh, the crunch is real,
Who knew decay could have such zeal?

As dusk unfolds, they sing and sway,
Forget about the wind's cruel play.
The ground becomes their warm embrace,
A leafy laugh, a final chase!

Unseen Journeys of the Leaf

A leaf once dreamed of flying far,
To dance with clouds and own a car.
"I'll hitch a ride on that bold bee!"
She squeaked with glee, "Come fly with me!"

But bees just buzzed, too busy, zippy,
While she sat stuck, oh so trippy.
"Maybe I'll float on a cozy breeze,
Join a flock of wandering leaves!"

She tried to catch a ride on fate,
To see the world, oh it felt great!
But each gust of wind was a letdown,
She just spun 'round, lost her crown.

Finally, she sighed, with a twist and curl,
Atop a frog, who gave a whirl.
With a giggle, they jumped from spot to spot,
A happy leaf, at last, why not?

Interwoven Tales in Twilight

At dusk the leaves all start to weave,
Their stories shared, they never leave.
One's a tale of a fateful flight,
The others laugh—what a silly sight!

"I took a dip in the pond so blue,
But came back soggy, how about you?"
Another shimmies, "I took the plunge,
In a wild wind, I did a lunge!"

"Oh dear, the funny things we prove!
Like when I tumbled, too much groove!"
A chorus chuckles under the stars,
Swapping their tales from Venus to Mars.

So twilight glimmers with what they say,
Tangled tales to end the day.
And through the night, with friendly cheer,
The leaves stay close, their laughter clear!

Rustle and Revel

Oh, listen close, the leaves convene,
In twirls and swirls, a dance routine!
With every rustle, giggles arise,
As they shake loose, under night skies.

One leaf boasts, "I'm quite the star,
At parties, I steal the jar!"
Another replies, "You mean the show?
I fell from the tree, put on a glow!"

They sway with glee, the moon shines bright,
In rustle and revel, pure delight.
The branches share secrets so spry,
While crickets join in, oh me, oh my!

So let's not fret, as autumn's here,
These leaves will dance, have no fear!
For in their laughter, life they savor,
An endless joy; nature's favor!

Rustling Memories

In the trees where whispers sigh,
Squirrels plan their heist up high.
They scurry, dash, and then they prance,
Stealing nuts with daring dance.

Fronds flutter like chipmunk tails,
Each breeze tells a tale that fails.
A leaf slips, makes a comic scene,
Nature's laugh—oh, how it's keen!

Twirling down, a beauty gray,
Leaves argue on who'll reign today.
Whirling around, they trip and flip,
A leafy watch: the clumsy trip!

In this chaos, joy takes flight,
Each rustle giggles through twilight.
Laughter sewn 'neath every bough,
Memory's roots, let's dance right now.

Veins of the Forest

Drawing lines on verdant skin,
Wiggly paths where critters spin.
Each twig a route, a zig-zag race,
While the old oak grins in its place.

Leaves feign seriousness and sway,
Yet scatterbrained at play all day.
One drifts slow, like a sleepy nurse,
While another mocks, saying "Who's worse?"

A lizard laughs at shadows cast,
Cheeky fun, this game will last.
Up and down, they dance so spry,
In the forest, never shy!

With each rustle, laughter grows,
Roots entwined in jokes, who knows?
Nature's veins pulse with delight,
A funny forest, pure and bright!

Nature's Mosaic

Colors scatter, reds and greens,
Painted leaves with quirky scenes.
A patchwork quilt across the ground,
In this chaos, joy is found!

Loudly snap a twig, a crack,
Nature winks, and then it's back.
"Who's stepping on my royal robe?"
A leaf grumbles in its abode.

Puddle splashes are a treat,
Dancing fairies with tiny feet.
Each squishy thump sends laughter skyward,
Little giggles from the birdward.

In this artwork, chaos swirls,
Fun unravels as nature twirls.
With every prance and rustling way,
The world's a circus, come what may!

The Language of Leaves

Whispers flutter, rustling news,
A gossipy realm in sunlit hues.
"Did you see that squirrel's big snack?"
"Please, he'll choke and fall right back!"

Leaves laugh softly, sharing tricks,
Their gossiping, a casual mix.
"It's too sunny; watch me frown!"
"Not at all, let's twirl around!"

The tickling breeze lifts spirits high,
As plants dance under a big blue sky.
A joke exchanged on every branch,
In this green scene, all take a chance!

In the end, every leaf and twig,
Turns the mundane into a jig.
Nature speaks in playful tone,
Each rustling breath, a joy we've grown.

The Dance of Decay

Leaves tumble down in a swirl,
They laugh and spin, join the whirl.
Old branches creak, a silly song,
They dance along, where they belong.

Squirrels chuckle, gathering snacks,
While acorns play hide and seek, no cracks.
A breeze gives a shimmy, quite the sight,
As nature groves under the moonlight.

Frayed Edges of Growth

In the garden, things get wild,
Weeds pop up, none are mild.
Petunias giggle, petals askew,
While daisies chuckle in morning dew.

A cactus wears a tiny hat,
It's fashion week for flora, imagine that.
Jack's bean stalks reach for the sky,
But get tangled up, oh my, oh my!

Sunlight Between the Trees

Sunbeams peek through leafy hats,
Tickling the woods and all the chats.
The shadows play tricks, hide and seek,
You can hear the trees giggle, so to speak.

Branches stretch, they wave hello,
While mushrooms giggle down below.
The squirrels discuss a grand design,
A picnic planned just after nine.

Patchwork of Seasons

Autumn wears a patchy coat,
With colors bright, it tries to float.
Spring giggles with a budding sprout,
While winter rolls in, but pouts about.

Summer's sun, a lazy tease,
Rests on grass and skips with ease.
The seasons chat, a lively crowd,
In nature's quilt, all wrapped, so proud.

Choreography of the Canopy

The branches sway, oh what a dance,
Leaves twist and twirl at every chance.
A squirrel jumps in a twinkling show,
Yet trips on a twig, and down he goes!

Sunshine giggles through the leafy roof,
As shadows play coy, a sly little proof.
Bugs form a band, buzzing in glee,
While the owl just naps, sipping on tea.

The wind plays a tune, a rustling tune,
Conducted by breezes that howl at the moon.
Each leaf a dancer, their moves quite a sight,
Even the acorns join in the flight!

In this grand show, nature takes her charge,
With branches that wave, oh so large.
A whimsical scene, full of cheer,
In this canopy dance, we all want a beer!

Enigmas in the Understory

In the lowlands, something's afoot,
A raccoon is playing hide-and-seek, who'd have thought?
Beneath tangled greens, a mystery brews,
Is that a gnome? No, just someone's shoes!

Mushrooms gossip, with dots and spots,
While ferns giggle in their laughing knots.
A worm thinks he's clever, a true little sneak,
But his wiggle in the dirt can't hide the squeak.

Leaves whisper secrets, shh, keep it low,
As the ants march by in quite the row.
Who's leading this crew? A dancing beetle,
With a tiny top hat, it's really quite regal!

In the underbrush, laughter takes flight,
As critters concoct tales deep in the night.
For life is a riddle, wrapped up in cheer,
In this leafy realm, it's all quite clear!

Petals and Shadows

Petals flutter like gossiping friends,
Swinging in breezes that never quite ends.
A daisy winks, oh what a flirt,
While the roses just roll, complaining of dirt.

Meanwhile, the shadows plot their parade,
Dancing on sidewalks, making a trade.
A butterfly zooms, caught in the game,
But soon finds out, it's lost its name.

Tulips are prancing in colors so bold,
While weeds throw confetti, or so I'm told.
The sunbeam giggles, a playful tease,
While petals surrender to the light breeze.

In this garden, humor takes root,
With laughter blooming, oh so astute.
So join in the fun, let's laugh, let's cheer,
In this patch of joy, there's nothing to fear!

A Leaf's Lament

Oh, the tales I tell from my lofty post,
Once a vibrant green, now I'm a ghost.
Drifting down softly, I dance with the breeze,
Only to land by a swarm of hungry bees!

Once I was proud, in the sunlight I shone,
Now I'm a crinkle, a crispy old bone.
The children all laugh, tossing me high,
While I reminisce about the days I could fly.

The trees now chuckle, oh what a sight,
As I tell them my stories, they twinkle with light.
But alas! Here I lie, with the dirt and the mud,
Trying to keep humor, in this leaf-shaped dud.

But I'll not despair, for who knows, my friend,
Maybe I'll sprout again, on that you can depend.
So here's to the laughter, the leaves in the park,
In each little heart, shines a spark!

Snippets of Life in a Leaf's Embrace

In a pile of leaves, I took a dive,
Squirrels chattered, as if they connive.
A gust of wind blew my hat away,
Who needs it, when trees dance and sway?

A ladybug waltzed, on a twig so thin,
With a wink and a nod, she spun her spin.
I tried to join in, but tripped on a vine,
The leaf laughed at me, 'You still look divine!'

Sunshine peeked through the leafy mane,
Whispering secrets of joy and pain.
Frogs serenaded beneath the blue,
As I collected moments, like a playful crew.

So here's to the laughter that nature brings,
To the leafy masks of our silly flings.
Embrace the absurd, let the giggles flow,
For in a leaf's embrace, we steal the show.

Sunlit Paths of Decaying Beauty

Upon the sunlit path, I strolled and giggled,
With butterflies flapping, I felt quite wiggled.
A worm in a tux, he tipped his top hat,
I wished him good luck in his fashionable spat.

The sun-drenched daisies chimed with delight,
"Why chase the clouds when the ground feels alright?"
A grumpy old toad sat, pondering life,
He mumbled about trouble and his nagging wife.

Leaves crunched beneath me; a symphony played,
Nature's own chorale in a floral parade.
A shade-loving grasshopper, he took my hand,
"Let's dance on the path; it's a leaf littered land!"

So I swayed with the critters in that rugged groove,
The sunset was watching, it dared to move.
In the beauty of decay, we find laughter and cheer,
For every fading petal, brings memories near.

Lush Dreams of the Woodland Realm

In a forest thick, where the whispers play,
A chipmunk recited his poetry today.
With acorns for props, he put on a show,
I laughed so hard, the mushrooms did glow!

The trees held their breath, in the soft, warm air,
As a feathered bard chirped tales without care.
He sang of mischief, of friends and of foes,
While a deer in the back tried to mimic his prose.

The sprinkle of sunlight danced on my nose,
As I stepped on a twig, oh how it froze!
A fox passed by, with a wink and a grin,
"Join our woodland party; let the fun begin!"

So we danced under branches, in shadows and light,
With giggles and gleeful twirls in the night.
In lush woodland dreams, we all found our spark,
For laughter's the magic, that ignites the dark.

Secrets Woven in the Underbrush

In the cozy underbrush, secrets reside,
Where a rabbit once lost a race and then cried.
"Too many blueberries on the trail," he pouted,
While ants gathered round, feeling quite crowded.

A possum played dead to avoid the debate,
While critters conspired on their sugary fate.
"Let's raid the picnic," said the sneaky crow,
But the humans had snacks, they couldn't forego!

Beneath tangled roots, a party occurs,
With fungi and flowers, and chirping of spurs.
A hedgehog proposed a game of charades,
"Don't prick your friends, let's not go off the blades!"

Giggles erupted with each twist and turn,
As the underbrush whispered what they could learn.
In nature's cocoon, joy swells without rush,
For secrets abound in the wild, oh so plush.

The Language of Withering Petals

When daisies gossip in the breeze,
They spill their tales with such great ease.
A sunflower shrugs, quite pompous too,
"I do not wilt, I'm just passing through!"

The rose rolls its eyes, tired of the chat,
"What is your secret? You look like a brat!"
The violets chuckle, dressed in their gowns,
"Just embrace your aging, don't wear frowns!"

Leaves dance on branches, twirling with flair,
"We've seen it all, like a nature fair!"
The marshmallow clouds drop jokes from above,
"We're all just fluff under stars that we love!"

So plant a garden ripe with your cheer,
Let nature giggle, let laughter be clear!
With each fade and twist of a petal's delight,
We bloom in our humor, so silly and bright!

Transient Greens in the Gloaming

In twilight whispers, greens take a stand,
Claiming forage rights on this soft land.
Rascally weeds throw a party quite mad,
"Join us, dear flowers, don't look so sad!"

They tip their hats, in stripes and in curls,
Moss giggles softly, "Such fun! What a world!"
The oak starts to chuckle, roots deep with pride,
"I've seen crazier things since my youth I bide!"

With crickets as DJs, the dance floor erupts,
As fireflies twinkle and laughter erupts.
The moon rolls its eyes, a glow in a swirl,
"These greens are bonkers, oh, what a whirl!"

So let's revel under the fading light,
Where greens get together and jive through the night.
In each fleeting moment, in shades that we glean,
Nature is laughing, forever serene!

Threads of Beauty from the Earth's Heart

Beneath the soil where critters moan,
Lie threads of wonders, gems overgrown.
Worms tell the tales of long-lost friends,
"Don't worry about leaves; they all make amends!"

Roots whisper softly of hidden delight,
"Sticks and stones may collide in the night!"
The daisies nod, with their heads held high,
"We're only here to wave at the sky!"

The grass plays a fiddle, strings made of dew,
While spiders spin webs of fantastical view.
"Join in, join in! Let's dance on this plot!"
Even thorns join the fun, despite their own lot!

So dig in the dirt, let the laughter seep,
From valleys to mountaintops, secrets to keep.
Nature's threads weave a tapestry bright,
Finished in giggles, oh, what a sight!

Tales Woven in Every Leaf

Each leaf has a secret it's eager to share,
"This summer was wild, full of good air!"
The maple grins broadly, saying with glee,
"Just wait 'til autumn, you'll all come to me!"

The birch rolls its bark, a jester so bold,
Whispers, "Get ready, my colors are gold!"
The fir sings a tune of evergreen dreams,
While squirrels on branches plot whimsical schemes!

With acorns debating the best way to fall,
A show of absurdity, laughter for all.
"Let's trip the humans with our sneaky dive,
They'll think they are wise, but we're so alive!"

So next time you wander where leaves weave a tale,
Listen for chuckles in the verdant veil.
From buds to old ages, through giggles we peep,
Nature's full of stories, so let's dive in deep!

Emojis of the Earth

Leaves waving like tiny hands,
Nature's applause for life's grand plans.
A pebble laughs, a twig does a dance,
All in sync, they take their chance.

Squirrels with acorns, a playful sight,
Nuts and giggles in morning light.
Grass tickles toes with its green embrace,
While daisies wink, in their flower space.

Clouds above play peek-a-boo,
While shadows stretch, just like me and you.
Nature's selfie, a picture of cheer,
Making us laugh, bringing good vibes here.

In this funny world, all's connected,
Listen closely, the earth's detected.
Every petal, every stone,
Tells a joke, so we're never alone.

Dappled Light and Memory

Sunbeams play on the forest floor,
Lighting up mushrooms with tales of yore.
A squirrel narrates its nutty quest,
While shadows giggle, they know best.

Flickering patches dance on leaves,
As trees gossip about who believes.
The breeze tells secrets, half whispered,
While the roots chuckle, ever crisper.

A friendly worm wears a leafy cap,
Tap dancing critters join in the clap.
Dappled light, a playful glow,
Nature's comedy, always on show.

Memories woven in each green thread,
With laughter ringing, spirits are fed.
In this theatre of vibrant dreams,
Laughter flows like bubbling streams.

Tinctures of Wilderness

In the wild, colors swirl and blend,
Nature's palette, never to end.
A deer wears spots like paint on a wall,
While clouds hug the hills, having a ball.

Berries chuckle when plucked with glee,
While vines twist about, as if to agree.
The wind whispers pranks in leafy ears,
And dandelions laugh away our fears.

A frog croaks jokes in a pond nearby,
While mosquitoes buzz in their frantic fly.
Nature's concoction, wild and free,
Mixing laughter in every tree.

The colors whisper, so bright, so bold,
Tinctures of wilderness, stories told.
In this raucous space, we've found our stripe,
With humor wrapped in nature's hype.

The Soul of the Forest Floor

Underneath the trees, a party unfolds,
With critters discussing their nature's gold.
Moss throws a blanket on the ground,
While mushrooms gather, making their sound.

Raccoons in masks, clever and sly,
Telling tall tales under the sky.
The soil hums a friendly tune,
As acorns roll like a festive boon.

A ladybug laughs, spots dancing around,
While roots kick back, feeling profound.
In this vibrant inn where stories mix,
Each leaf a character, with silly tricks.

The forest floor, a whimsical stage,
Capturing memories, page by page.
With laughter echoing, so light and pure,
The humor of nature, oh so sure.

www.ingramcontent.com/pod-product-compliance
Lightning Source LLC
Chambersburg PA
CBHW072144200426
43209CB00051B/457